The Family Economy

The Family Economy

Discovering the Family as It Was Designed to Work

by RORY GROVES

Afterword by Allan C. Carlson

WIPF & STOCK · Eugene, Oregon

THE FAMILY ECONOMY
Discovering the Family as It Was Designed to Work

Wipf & Stock
An Imprint of Wipf and Stock Publishers
199 W. 8th Ave., Suite 3
Eugene, OR 97401

www.wipfandstock.com

PAPERBACK ISBN: 979-8-3852-1238-5
HARDCOVER ISBN: 979-8-3852-1239-2
EBOOK ISBN: 979-8-3852-1240-8

VERSION NUMBER 02/23/24

Unless otherwise indicated, all Scripture quotations are from The ESV®
Bible (The Holy Bible, English Standard Version®), copyright © 2001 by
Crossway, a publishing ministry of Good News Publishers. Used by per-
mission. All rights reserved.

Scripture quotations marked KJV are taken from the The King James Version.

for Evergreen

*What therefore God hath joined together,
let not man put asunder.*

—St. Mark 10:9 (KJV)

Contents

Introduction

Unthinkable Again

When you destroy the given order of the family, you, in short,
destroy both the life and the family. An apple tree chainsawed
to the ground and then stacked next to the wall as cordwood
hardly remains an apple tree, or any sort of tree for that matter
. . . . It will never again bear what gave it its identity—apples.

—BLAIR ADAMS, *WHAT KIND OF FAMILY?*

IT IS SAID THAT when men first started to leave the farm to work in the mines, their families followed. After centuries of working the same ground together, generation after generation, it was unthinkable that a job should separate a man from his wife, a father from his children, a family from its home.

Families worked together. That's how it had always been, and that's how it always would be. Or so they thought.

For most of history, the family economy was the unifying force in human culture—the cement of civilization. Until very recently this societal arrangement was natural, enduring, and unquestioned. It could be evidenced even in the earliest stages of industrialism when whole families were hired to operate textile factories in what came to be known as "family mills." Even as late as the Civil War, it was not uncommon to find soldiers living with their families in military camps.

So when fathers left for the mines, their families came with. They made their homes nearby, prepared meals together, washed laundry together, reared and educated their children, all around the mouth of the cave that swallowed their father daily, from sun up to sun down.

Eventually children were brought into the mines, and factories too, and fitted to tasks deemed suitable for little hands: tasks that bright, young children were only eager to do to win the admiration of their daddy (like days on the farm). Tasks such as opening a mule cart door for twelve hours a day, six days a week, five hundred feet underground. Wives and daughters were brought into the textile mills where, they were told, they would be "more useful than they otherwise would be" at home.[1]

This newfound way of work was welcomed by some and resisted by many, but it was here to stay. "The general industrial growth of communities was . . . an irresistible though a slowly coming tide," historians would note. "Progressive methods of employment and the introduction of machinery gradually broke down all opposition."[2]

It was the Age of Prosperity and rising standards of living. The Industrial Revolution demanded, above all, efficiency. And nothing is more inefficient than human relationships.

So, after thousands of years of historical practice, families stopped working together. They left self-sustaining farms

1. Bureau of Labor Statistics, *History of Wages*, 85.
2. Allen, *Shoe Industry*, 21.

for jobs in the city. They exchanged generational lands for rented tenements. They traded time together for paychecks apart. And the unbroken cycle of father and son, of mother and daughter, of family and home was put asunder.

Within a few generations family function and integrity would devolve to a state unrecognizable to the preindustrial world. And the rising tide has not abated since: the cement which binds us is crumbling and washing out to sea.

This book is for families who are ready to turn the tide. It is for fathers who do not want to spend the majority of their waking lives separated from their families. It is for wives who desire connection with their husbands and vision for their homes. It is for parents who are tired of watching their children grow and mature and abandon the way of life they hold so dear.

In the flood of fragmentation, this study explores a way forward.

In the chapters that follow, I outline the historical developments that led to fractured families of today. But I do not mean to merely articulate the problems, of which we are all well aware. After years of writing and teaching on the family economy, I wanted something practical that I could put into people's hands, something that both introduces the concept and provides initial steps for those wanting to get started.

All is not lost; indeed, there is much reason for hope. We are reaching a critical moment in the West. An historic moment. Some commentators have said that the next few years will be remembered as the most significant since the fall of Rome. How we respond to these challenges will be felt for generations. We needn't remain as fractured families and splintered communities. There exists an opportunity to right the ship, to turn the tide.

There was a time when separating the family in order to subsist would have been unthinkable. Let us make it unthinkable again.

Rory Groves
December 2023

"Their families followed." 31st Pennsylvania Infantry, Fort Bunker Hill. 1861. (Photo: Library of Congress)

PART I

Principles

1

Put Asunder

A clear and ancient harmony
Pierces my soul through all its din,
As through its utmost melody—
Farther behind than they, farther within.

—Henry David Thoreau, "Inspiration"

Among the various signs that portend a serious, life-threatening emergency—heart attack, stroke, fatal poisoning—there is a symptom which, if it presents at all, presents first. Before chest pains or heart palpitations or any other physiological signs of stress, a patient may harbor intense feelings that "something bad is about to happen." On the surface, everything may appear to be normal. Healthy, even. But underneath, critical systems are failing and the patient's very life may be in peril. There are times when the only evidence doctors have to go on is this symptom, clinically known as "a sense of impending doom."

At first glance one might wonder what, if anything, could possibly be wrong with the society in which we find ourselves. By most accounts, we live in the most prosperous era of the most prosperous nation that has ever existed. The average citizen today has nearly instant access to an infinite supply of goods and services. We can transport ourselves to any part of the planet in a matter of hours. Food is abundant and cheap. Water flows at the push of a lever, lights appear at the flick of a switch. We think nothing of the garbage that is collected or sewage that is pumped to treatment plants miles away. Appliances do the dirty work in our homes while limitless entertainment is streamed on-demand into every room. In our cities, concrete and steel soar to the skies as a monument to human industry and ingenuity. And schools and hospitals and shopping malls and stadiums accent the landscape in all directions.

Every human impulse has been satisfied, it would seem, or is on the way to being satisfied. And yet, underneath it all, there remains a nagging unease—a foreboding that "pierces our souls." Through the numbing of our screens and analgesics, the ancient alarm rings for those who still have ears to hear: something has gone horribly wrong.

Yes, there are threats to our liberties, soaring debt and inflation, creeping tyranny, and increasingly polarized public (and private) discourse. There are technological and biological threats. There are wars and rumors of wars. But behind all of that there is something deeper. Something more elemental. To understand it, we have to look back.

GAINING THE WHOLE WORLD

Some revolutions are visible only in hindsight. Americans of the early nineteenth century didn't know they were fighting a revolution; they thought the revolution was over. And yet this undeclared war—this *Industrial Revolution*—would permanently alter our relationship with work, with tradition, and with each other. Relentless innovation combined with "progressive methods of employment" delivered unprecedented material abundance and rising standards of living. So rapid and far-reaching was the advance of the "factory system" that it is regarded by many historians as "the most important event in the history of humanity since the domestication of animals and plants, perhaps the most important since the invention of language."[1]

But our prosperity came at a price. All of the newfound abundance was predicated on the efficient allocation of *human* capital. Work was specialized and workers divided in order to mass-produce—workers, even, from the same family. Centuries later, is it any wonder we find the family more divided than it has been at any point in human history?

"The triumph of industrialism brought a 'great disruption' or a 'great transformation' in human affairs," writes Allan C. Carlson in *The Natural Family*:

> The creation of wealth accelerated under the regime of industry. Yet this real gain rested on tearing productivity away from the hearth, on a disruption of the natural ecology of family life. The primal bond of home and work appeared to dissolve into air. Family-made goods and tasks became commodities, things to be bought and sold. Centralized factories, offices, and warehouses took over the tasks of the family workshop, garden, kitchen, and storeroom. Husbands, wives, and even children were enticed

1. McCloskey, Review of *Cambridge Economic History of Modern Britain*, §14.

out of homes and organized in factories according to the principle of efficiency.[2]

"TRIUMPH OF INDUSTRIALISM"

Much can be written about the unintended consequences of the Industrial Revolution—and much already has—but as it pertains to the disintegration of the family there have been five primary impacts:

Centralization: Farm to Factory

The "great transformation" of society did not merely move jobs from one locale to another. It altered our entire understanding of the household as a productive enterprise. As family members separated into centrally situated factories, the home ceased to be the primary means of sustenance. As a result, the driving force of family unity—shared productive labor—ceased to be a relevant influence by the end of the nineteenth century.

Wendell Berry tells of the tragic outcomes of the Scottish poet Edwin Muir's family, who resettled from generational lands to rented tenements: "For thirty centuries, everything had been pretty much the same. The literature of his boyhood was the ballads and the Bible and Robert Burns. And then his family picked up and moved to Glasgow, right into the middle of the industrial revolution. And several of them died! It's heartbreaking! They died of uprootedness. . . . All

---

2. Carlson and Mero, *Natural Family*, 6.

the way from the old, old tradition into the modern night-
mare, you might say."[3]

Rather than producers, as households have traditionally
been understood, we are now *consumers*, and increasingly
dependent on external economies, distant manufacturers,
and long—and fragile—supply chains to provide for our
basic needs. Whereas the home, itself, had once been the
principle "factory" of society, it stands now as a mere shell of
its former function and authority.

Families that divided into factories (and rarely into the
same factory) no longer educated or apprenticed their children at home, breaking the cycle of generational mentorship
that had been practiced in all previous generations. Government schools, private institutions, and, eventually, day-care
centers took over the primal obligations of educating and
rearing the young, according to industrial principles.

"The biggest single factor" for the weakening of family
ties since the seventeenth century according to historian John
Demos, "seems to have been the separation of work from the
individual household, in connection with the growth of an
urban, industrial system."[4]

Urbanization: Country to City

Cities and eventually metropolises grew up around these
centralized factories. The allure of easy money—and competition from industry—drove millions from generational
lands into urban centers. Between 1790 and 1850 the number of Americans living in cities jumped eighteen-fold,

3. Petrusich, "Going Home with Wendell Berry."
4. Demos, *Little Commonwealth*, 187.

from 200,000 to 3.6 million. Along with this mass migration came a fracturing of communitarian life that had for centuries maintained social order and cohesion. No longer would families and communities depend on each other in self-sustaining towns and villages. No longer would they grow their own food, nourish their own sick, resolve their own disputes, protect their own neighbors, aid their own impoverished, and, in times of crisis, replenish their own losses. Impersonal institutions such as corporations, courts, government bureaus, and insurance agents would now fill the void—for a price.

In sum, relationships were no longer paramount. In the contest between tradition and economic opportunity that urbanization represented, relationships lost. Life, liberty, and the pursuit of happiness ceased to be connected with, or contingent upon, maintaining trust and respect with one's neighbors—or even one's own family. And the timeless bonds of family and community began to loosen.

> If there is no household or community economy, then family members and neighbors are no longer useful to one another. When people are no longer useful to one another, the centripetal force of family and community fails, and people fall into dependence on exterior economies and organizations. The hegemony of professionals and professionalism erects itself on local failure, and from then on the locality exists merely as a market for consumer goods and as a source of "raw material," human and natural.[5]

5. Berry, *World-Ending Fire*, 112.

Not only were families severed from each other, urbanization meant that they were increasingly divorced from the land. Man's original commission to "tend and keep" creation was no longer requisite to survival. Every material want and need could be satisfied through intermediaries: general stores, mail-order catalogs, railways, and today, screens.

Specialization: Jack of All Trades to Master of None

At the time of our nation's founding, there were around seventy distinct occupations. Today there are over thirty thousand, with more being created—and destroyed—every day. Limiting one's abilities to discreet, specialized tasks is a hallmark of the factory system. Productive output soars as energies and attention are narrowed to one particular task. But so does dependence. The more specialized we become in our chosen occupations, the more dependent we become on external provision.

Historically, society was composed of generalists, more or less. The average man could erect a dwelling as readily as drive a team of oxen. "A most striking, yet commonly forgotten, attribute of the Puritan settlers in seventeenth-century Massachusetts was that all were farmers," writes Carlson. "Even pastors, shopkeepers, and artisans spent a substantial portion of their time tilling the soil and tending animals."[6]

These rudimentary, though wide-ranging, skillsets not only reinforced family and community bonds through cooperative labor, they also ensured stability in times of crisis. Foreign wars, government lockdowns, and fragile supply chains did not threaten the preindustrial family.

6. Carlson, *Family Cycles*, 5.

But perhaps the most devastating, and unexpected, consequence of specialization is the way it limits family involvement in one's vocation. Traditionally, all ages and both genders participated in shared labor, usually on a farm or in a trade. By the time children were six or seven years old, they were meaningfully engaged in the family enterprise, and often integral to it.[7] This meant, above all, *time together.* Mothers and daughters, fathers and sons, grandparents and grandchildren were rarely parted in former times. A glaring consequence of removing fathers from the home—one that has received much attention in social and psychological literature of the past century—has been the decline of paternal authority in the family, leading to what Alexander Mitscherlich calls a "society without the father." Author and poet Robert Bly explains:

> The traditional way of raising sons, which lasted for thousands and thousands of years, amounted to fathers and sons living in close—murderously close—proximity, while the father taught the son a trade: perhaps farming or carpentry or blacksmithing or tailoring. As I've suggested elsewhere, the love unit most damaged by the Industrial Revolution has been the father-son bond.[8]

7. For more on this see *A Little Commonwealth: Family Life in Plymouth Colony* by John Demos: "It is striking that the seventeenth century (indeed all centuries before our own) had no real word for the period of life between puberty and full manhood. The term 'adolescence' is little more than seventy-five years old, at least in the sense of having wide currency. . . . Childhood as we know it did not last much beyond the age of six or seven years. After that, participation in adult activities began in earnest. . . . Children spent most of their time working (and relaxing) alongside older people, and were generally perceived as 'little adults'. . . . At Plymouth the 'teens' formed a period of relatively calm and steady progress toward full maturity" (*Little Commonwealth*, 145, 182).

8. Bly, *Iron John*, 19.

There are very few vocations today which facilitate family-centered work (the subject of another book).[9] Seven-year-olds are unlikely to join mom at the bank teller's window. Nor can she help dad sling code on his laptop computer. The challenge with children today is to keep them occupied while mom and dad become productive contributors to The Economy—which is, of course, the purpose of public schooling.[10]

Mechanization: Becoming Tools of Our Tools

As our relationship with work changed, so did our relationship with technology. Since the advent of civilization, and even before that, people have employed tools to aid them in their work. After Adam and Eve left the garden, Cain became a "tiller of the soil." He probably wasn't doing that with his bare hands. But we can also acknowledge that tools may be employed for sinister purposes as well. When Cain killed his brother, he probably didn't do that with his bare hands either.

Aiding the "great transformation" wrought by the Industrial Revolution was a new attitude toward technology. The mechanization of labor meant that, for the first time in history, rather than machines being fitted to the needs of people, people would be fitted to machines. Considerations of human dignity and social cohesion became secondary factors in the pursuit of "faster and cheaper." Though it took

9. See *Durable Trades: Family-Centered Economies That Have Stood the Test of Time.*

10. Bly puts it thus: "The Industrial Revolution, in its need for office and factory workers, pulled fathers away from their sons and, moreover, placed the sons in compulsory schools where the teachers are mostly women" (*Iron John*, 19).

time, and there were certainly many detractors, eventually society succumbed to the materialist ideology: "more is better." As a result, as Thoreau put it, "men have become the tools of their tools."[11]

> The machine turns on us and claims its own rights. It needs less and less, while more and more of us are required to run it, till we end as mere extensions of the machine, without freedom, and deprived of our own nature.[12]

Now that people were being fitted to machines, women and even children could be incorporated into the grand industrial project. Dividing labor into rudimentary tasks meant that the corporate efforts of "factory girls" and untrained children could accomplish what hitherto required years of apprenticeship and the skill of master craftsmen. This allowed, even encouraged, the splitting apart of family members to an extent never before practiced, nor even conceived. Advertising campaigns began denigrating domestic duties and offering powerful financial incentives to lure daughters away from the home farm to work in factories. "The labor of the mills is considered much more honorable than the labor of domestic life," reads one editorial appearing in *Dwight's American Magazine and Family Newspaper* in 1846. "While in the mills a girl will earn more money, exclusive of her board, than can the ablest man on a farm."[13]

Women, in particular, were recruited in droves, and in droves they came. "During America's textile boom, young

11. Thoreau, *Walden*, 41.

12. Attributed to Lewis Mumford, author of *Myth of the Machine: Technics and Human Development*.

13. American Antiquarian Society, "Situation of the Lowell Girls."

women made up three-quarters of the workforce," according to historians. "They left their homes in distant farmlands aboard baggage-wagons. The age of the mill girls ranged from ten years old to middle age, although the majority of them were in their twenties."[14]

Mill Girl at Work. (Photo: Lewis Hine/Library of Congress)

Mechanization can be credited as the engine of the revolution. From 1815 to 1840 the output of textile products in New England increased a thousandfold, and the price of cloth dropped by at least 60 percent.[15] Many fortunes were made and some of America's first millionaires were minted during this period. But it begs the question: Were human beings designed to be cogs in a machine?

Francis Schaeffer writes,

14. American Antiquarian Society, "Who Were the Mill Girls?," §1.

15. National Bureau of Economic Research, "Total Cotton Production by Mills in New England"; Shammas, "Decline of Textile Prices," 483–507.

> The Bible presents to us no mechanical human rela-
> tionships; it allows none, because God did not make
> us as machines. . . . Every man is my neighbor and
> is to be treated in a proper human, man-to-man re-
> lationship. Every time we act in a machinelike way
> towards another man we deny the central teaching
> of the Word of God—that there is a personal God
> who has created man in his own image.[16]

Regardless of the abundance it created or the useful (or useless) inventions it sired, mechanization reshaped all of society according to the image of industry. And for many families, that meant the end of the home economy as a viable way of life.

Atomization: Social to Solitary

The Industrial Revolution was, first and foremost, a revolution of ideas. The aforementioned shifts, once established, gave rise to new philosophies and mindsets that would have been inconceivable in tight-knit communities of previous eras. From Karl Marx and Frederich Engels came the deification of the State and incursions into the private sphere: "The education of all children from the moment that they can get along without a mother's care, shall be in state institutions," Engels declared in *Principles of Communism*.[17] From Charles Darwin came the theory of evolution, which interpreted biological life not as purposefully designed but as a series of continuous, goal-oriented improvements from lower life forms to higher. Social theorists soon applied this logic in their own field and began challenging every historical

16. Schaeffer, *True Spirituality*, 132–33.

17. Engels, *Principles of Communism*, 18:viii.

tradition and social institution that came before as inferior, including the family.

But before either of these powerful philosophies were loosed, there was another that preceded and, indirectly, enabled them. "In the field of economics," writes historian Carle C. Zimmerman in *Family and Civilization*, "the theory of the free and unrestrained individual arose. This individual was to challenge every value in relation to his profit, loss, and gain in material consumption."[18]

A defining characteristic of the last two hundred years has been the slow but steady decline of social attachments to family and community in conjunction with a rise in economic independence. Sociologists refer to this process as "individualization" or the "atomization" of a society. And it has happened—and still is happening—in every industrialized nation of the world.

Whereas the family economy once incentivized cooperative labor at home, or locally with neighbors, the industrial economy now incentivizes individual achievement in a global, impersonal, marketplace. Whereas life in community—life *for* community—once shaped our ambitions, wants, and needs, multinational corporations now whet (and satiate) our individual appetites. Whereas familial independence and generational mentorship once served as the basis for one's work, the new gospel is mammon. It is an economy rooted not in cooperation and trust, but in competition and envy.

"The Pilgrims saw the world in terms of groups—family, church, community, nation," Robert Tracy McKenzie points out:

18. Zimmerman, *Family and Civilization*, 124.

Whatever we think of their view, the contrast drives home our own preoccupation with the individual. The individual is now the constituent unit of American society, individual fulfillment holds sway as the highest good, individual conscience reigns as the highest authority. We conceive of adulthood as the absence of all accountability, define liberty as the elimination of all restraint, and measure the worth of social organizations—labor unions, clubs, political parties, even churches—by the degree to which they promote our individual agendas.[19]

As American theologians Stanley Hauerwas and William Willimon put it, "Our society is a vast supermarket of desire, in which each of us is encouraged to stand alone and go out and get what the world owes us."[20]

The dominance of economic individualism can be seen all around. Never before in human history have people been able to live so isolated from each other. Never before have we been able to subsist wholly detached from our families and outside of community. For thousands of years we worked and worshiped and feasted and mourned together. But today, everything we need can be procured from a store or screen, without ever having to make eye contact.

"Atomization creates the perfect individual for the industrial corporate order," says Carlson. "The desire, however sometimes sublimated, is for persons without close human relations or skills . . . . The atomized, consuming individual is actually the anthropological goal of an advanced industrial system."[21]

---

19. McKenzie, "How the Pilgrims' Story," §§3–4.
20. Hauerwas and Willimon, *Resident Aliens*, 77.
21. Carlson, letter to the author, July 31, 2023.

TWILIGHT OF THE FAMILY

And so, centuries later, we find ourselves wrestling through a paradox of wealth and loss, of abundance and loneliness. Are these merely superficial symptoms? Or early omens of a culture-wide emergency? The "atomistic family" that is common today, according to Zimmerman, has not been seen since the waning days of the Roman Empire, before the world plunged into the first Dark Age.

Our prosperity, it turns out, is measured solely in material terms; relationally we are destitute. Familial and communal bonds are a mere shadow of what for centuries defined productive households and resilient communities: marriages are failing, fertility is plummeting, generational faith is imploding, mental disorders are epidemic, and despair deaths are soaring. "Rich nations dominate the list of countries most burdened by the full range of mental illnesses," according to international research.[22] And suicide is now the second-leading cause of death for adolescents in America.[23] This is the price we are paying for gaining the whole world.

We are left with the question: In the face of such monumental shifts, corrupt philosophies, and entrenched interests, what can one family possibly do? Quite a bit, actually. The answer, I believe, can only come from families, and it can only start at home. Despite the consequences of modernity, "through all its din," the ancient harmony still rings for those who will listen: We must go back to where we left the path. Not to a previous era, or a primitive mode of living, but to an ancient way of thinking.

---

22. Institute for Health Metrics, "Global Burden of Disease."
23. CDC, "Facts about Suicide."

If God, when joining men and women in holy matrimony, commanded, "Let not man separate," is it possible that he meant that command to extend to our families as well?

The crisis of our time will not be remedied by electing the right politicians, attaining enough education, stockpiling enough food, or amassing enough wealth. Our vast prosperity came at the expense of relational integrity. And the only way to recover relational wealth in our families and communities is to return to the age-old pattern—I would venture, *biblical pattern*—of working together.

It's time to rebuild the family economy.

2

Joined Together

*This triangle of truisms, father, mother, and child cannot be
destroyed; it can only destroy civilisations which disregard it.*

—G. K. CHESTERTON

QUITE OFTEN, AFTER GIVING a talk at a conference or workshop, I will be approached by someone, usually a father, with
a wild look in his eye. It is the look of a man with whom the
idea of the family economy has resonated, but he sees no way
to get there—as though he has caught a glimpse of the Prom-
ised Land but there is an impassible sea before him. Often he
comes with the singular question: "How?"

The problem with a question like this is that there is no
pat answer. What worked for one family will not necessarily
work for another. While there are common principles which
I review in the next chapter, each family is unique, and each
family must discover their own path to wholeness. I believe,
in fact, that this is entirely the point. When the seas are parted for your family it comes with a testimony: ". . . that the
next generation might know them, the children yet unborn,

and arise and tell them to their children, so that they should set their hope in God and not forget the works of God, but keep his commandments."[24]

So rather than attempt a formula, I will simply share our story. And perhaps you can find yourself somewhere therein.

THE SMALLEST OF SEEDS

Our first foray into a family-centered economy started, oddly enough, with a tomato plant on our apartment balcony. We were living, in many ways, the typical American consumer life: we bought our food at the grocery store, sported fashions from the mall, and shopped for most everything else at supercenters.

My wife, Becca, was working for a youth camp in Nebraska while I was managing a software startup in Omaha. We were apart for most of the day, often reuniting after work for a fast-food dinner and a few hours of television before going to bed and repeating it all over again the next day. We didn't have much in the way of attachments—no kids, no yard, no relatives nearby. Just the apartment. And a cat.

The tomato plant presented a bit of an encumbrance—to me, anyway. Now I had an obligation, something to tend. It wasn't even my idea: someone gave it to Becca as a gift. And now here it was, taking up space on my balcony. Little did I realize that the humble vine would change the course of our lives. Like the smallest of seeds that grows into a mighty tree.

I watched with curiosity as green leaves unfurled and sprouted little yellow blossoms, which then bulged into tiny green berries, and finally, red ripe tomatoes. My curiosity

24. Ps 78:6–7.

turned to wonder as I tasted our very first homegrown tomato. If this was food, what had we been eating?

Becca made bruschetta out of the meager harvest, and BLTs—what she refers to as the "trifecta of food." The little tomato plant was soon joined by basil and bell peppers and whatever else we could fit on a five-by-eight-foot balcony.

But it wasn't only the plants that were growing. Something was taking root inside of us too.

The experiment on our apartment balcony led to a full-fledged love of gardening and a desire to become more self-sufficient. We soon found ourselves on a tiny lot in the city, replacing most of the yard with raised bed gardens and tearing out the decorative landscaping to plant raspberry canes. We pored over homesteading books in the evenings and began to dream together about what life on the land might look like. It was about the time that we were looking into city ordinances for keeping chickens that we decided we needed more space—and looser zoning regulations.

Our second child was nine days old when we packed the U-Haul and moved to a rural farm in southern Minnesota (an eventful week for Becca). At the time, our desire was mainly to enjoy the country life: to plant a larger garden, raise some chickens. Maybe even a goat. In other words, to "hobby farm." I had no intention of changing careers; I had worked many years to build a viable software business, and I wasn't about to hang that up to sell eggs.

But something happened that we never saw coming. In the process of planting tomatoes and tending chickens and milking goats, we began to connect with an ancient way of life. We were raising food more or less the same way our great-grandparents did, and their parents before them, in a line that stretched all the way back to the First Parents.

My wife and I so enjoyed what we were learning that almost from the beginning we invited others to join in. We hosted maple tree–tapping parties and honeybee workshops and gave farm tours. To us, the ancient path was a fulfilling one, and we wanted to share it. We called our farm "A Learning Farm" because we were the ones learning. Every new skill was inspiring. Every animal a triumph. People came and learned alongside us. Hundreds of them, in fact. They were eager to learn, but also eager to meet others who were searching for another way forward.

Through this process of learning and growing and extolling the virtues of life on the land, something else was happening too: our family was working together. My job had always provided an income, but there had never been a way to include my family in this most central focus of my time. On the farm, however, everyone was needed, and everybody worked. Even our little ones had jobs: collecting eggs, digging potatoes, canning tomatoes with mom, or mending fences with dad. They named animals and bottle-fed lambs. Mostly they loved doing what we were doing, because we were doing it together.

We didn't realize it at the time, but as we were making a farm, our farm was making a family.

ALL IN THE HOUSE

A family economy, simply defined, is when a family works together to provide the things they need. As foreign of a concept as this appears to modern minds, it was in fact the usual way of things for most of human history. Prior to the Industrial Revolution, "every household was a self-producing and self-sustaining community."[25]

Of course, times were simpler then. Life did not consist in the abundance of possessions, like it does today. Most were content therewith having food and raiment. This is perhaps the fundamental difference, and what makes it so peculiar in our time: as opposed to a corporate economy, or an industrial economy, or a centrally planned economy, a family economy is concerned with relationships over possessions.

Complexity has brought us many wonderful inventions—like air conditioning and motor vehicles. But when times were simpler, families depended on each other, and other families in their community. There were no supermarket chains or fashion outlets. No fast food franchises or mega malls. One could not order replacement parts over the Internet and have them delivered to his door two days later. Families and communities relied on each other in order to survive. And nearly everyone survived directly off the produce of the land. In other words, they were *producers*.

From those First Parents up until the Industrial Revolution, this family-centric model served, with few exceptions, as the basis for civilization. This used to be common knowledge, as our language reflects. Our word for *economy* derives from the Greek *oikonomia*, meaning "household management" or "household law." "In the beginning," writes C. R. Wiley, "it was all in the house—the whole economy."[26]

Along with complexity came certain tradeoffs. Air conditioning keeps our homes cool, motor vehicles transport

25. Robinson, *Loom and Spindle*, 2.
26. Wiley, "Against the Recreational Household."

us faster and farther. But in order to have these things we must become dependent on producers outside our family and external to our community. This means we are no longer self-sufficient, nor even community-sufficient, but instead rely on a vast and intricate network of global manufacturing and just-in-time delivery—a network over which we have no control, delivering products which we had no hand in making, enabling a complete and utter ignorance of what went in to making them. In other words, we are *consumers*.

Consumption, on some level, is necessary—we all have to do it. But dependence is another matter. Thomas Jefferson warned, "Dependence begets subservience and venality, suffocates the germ of virtue, and prepares fit tools for the designs of ambition."[27]

But the greatest consequence of complexity and our consumerist mindset is not the loss of self-sufficiency or even sacred liberty, but *time together*. Our homes are cooler, but increasingly idle—and empty. Our transport is faster, but carries us away from the very people who matter most.

LIFE TOGETHER

In my own case, the contradiction was getting hard to ignore. Each morning, after finishing chores together, I would wave "goodbye" to my family as I went to work in my "real job," which consisted of sitting alone in an office all day, staring at a screen.

By contrast, everything we did on the farm was done together: tapping maple trees, baling hay, picking plums, chasing goats. The results of our labor were immediate and

---

27. Jefferson, *Notes on the State of Virginia*, 176.

tangible, not theoretical and abstract as I was used to in the world of high tech. We were eating chops and steaks from lambs we had pastured and eggs from chickens we had hatched and raised. The harvests were joyous and sustaining—they brought us closer together and fed us through the long Minnesota winters. The "hobby farm" was becoming more real than my "real job": it was the more integrated way to live and work.

Tomato Harvest. (Photo: Becca Groves)

The question burned in my mind: *Was it possible to live this way all the time?* To work alongside my family rather than be separated for the majority of my day? To put my hand towards something that was truly real, truly living—connected to creation and its Creator? If such a life were possible, then this was the life I wanted to spend the rest of my days living.

These questions led me to the writings of Allan Carlson, Kevin Swanson, C. R. Wiley, Blair Adams, and others. I would discover that not only was a family-centered vocation possible but that the family as a "work unit" was the normative pattern for most of human history. And the way we work today—in specialized careers—is the exception.

"The basic economic unit is not an individual and it is not a corporation or the government," writes Kevin Swanson in *Family Life*. "According to the creation mandate and 5,900 years of historical practice, the basic economic unit is the family."[28]

TURNING THE TIDE

Before we had language to describe it, we could observe the positive effects of working together: Our marriage took on new life, our children found purpose and place, we discovered new opportunities for discipleship and mentorship, and we learned how to be more self-reliant at home. After decades of divided labor, the fragmented pieces of our family began to fit together in ways we had never experienced before.

A Marriage Reborn

The first thing we noticed was how our marriage started to improve. My wife and I were no longer two individuals with separate career goals, interests, hobbies, and coworkers. We were no longer walking separate paths that gradually diverged into distance and detachment. Our paths were

28. Swanson, *Family Life*, 115.

merging into a shared vision for the whole family—a vision that extended beyond our lifetimes.

My role as a husband was given new purpose and sense of duty: I was not merely a means to a paycheck, I was the *paterfamilias*; the head of the household. Responsibility for the entirety of my family's well-being—physical, spiritual, and economic—fell to me. I needed direction to lead my family and sought God to supply it. Becca found new understanding and enthusiasm in her role as a *helpmeet*—making possible a dream that could never be realized alone and becoming, in the process, my closest confidant and truest friend.

For the first time in our marriage, the biblical admonition that "the two shall become one flesh" ceased to be a spiritual abstract. We were daily growing and converging into a single being, thinking and then acting in one accord.

Children on Purpose

As our marriage found renewed purpose, we started looking for ways to bring our children into the work. Every child comes with unique qualities—interests and aptitudes, strengths and weaknesses. We began to ask the questions: Why did God bring this particular child with these particular gifts—and these particular challenges—into our family? What did God intend that we do together that we could never do apart? And then we set about designing a family economy around the strengths, interests, and personalities of each member.

In times past, families did not wait until a child was eighteen before career considerations came into view. Nor did they rely upon high school guidance counselors or aptitude tests. Historically, the household economy served as the primary on-ramp to life and career. Children as young as three years old were beginning to engage in the family business: collecting eggs, minding geese, cleaning the workshop, and, crucially, imitating whatever mom and dad were doing. By the time a child was seven or eight, he was exhibiting aptitudes for a particular trade, which his parents were wise to nurture. By twelve or thirteen he was apprenticing under a master craftsman, well on his way to establishing a viable household economy for his own family someday.

Though a few centuries removed, we have seen a similar pattern in our own family. My oldest son, Ivar, manages the livestock on our farm. Since he was old enough to hold a pitchfork, he joined his daddy in the work of herding, watering, feeding, and fencing. Eventually the day came, when I estimated his abilities sufficient, that I handed the reins over to him. And Ivar has diligently filled this role every day since, freeing me up to focus on other endeavors. We still work together often (particularly when loading hogs), and I'm only a stone's throw away when he needs me. But I can truly say that we would not be as successful in farming or effective in ministry without Ivar. This twelve-year-old boy is indispensable to our family economy.

The same could be said for each of our other children. Each one makes a unique contribution without which we could not do what we are doing. Even our decision to have more children was influenced by the awareness that God has a purpose and place for each one, and a vision that could not be realized without them. Each child gives us a glimpse into the calling God has for our family. And through our family economy, our children get a glimpse of what God has in mind for theirs.

Ivar may not decide to become a professional herdsman, but that is beside the point. Whether he chooses to become a doctor, lawyer, woodworker, or microbiologist, Ivar will know how to grow his own food, build his own home, maintain his own equipment, and work with his own family. And so will my grandchildren.

A Productive Household

Now that we were pursuing economy together, we came to view even our home differently—as a center of production rather than merely for rest and recreation.

Tour any portion of our farm and you are likely to find gardens growing, chickens laying, orchards bearing, bees buzzing, sap evaporating, firewood splitting, stoves heating, sourdough proving, herbs drying, manure pitching, wood working, wool weaving, sheep grazing, goats breaking, dad mending, mom teaching, and family worshiping.

So many of these traditional household functions have been removed to factory floors, commercial farms, supermarkets, and specialty stores. But historically, these were the kinds of activities that families engaged in together, and home was where they practiced them. Naturally, living on a farm affords more opportunity for enterprise—and I will say that a farm is more ideally suited to family enterprise than any other arrangement—but it's not a prerequisite. In a very real sense, that potted tomato plant on our apartment balcony was the beginning of home production in our family.

Fortress of Family

The productive home also proves resilient in times of trouble. We had been working together, growing our own food and developing skills for several years when COVID emerged as a global concern. Through all of the lockdowns, mandates, and supply chain shortages, it was business as usual on the homestead: we had jobs that nobody could cancel, we had gardens to tend and cellars stocked when grocery store shelves ran empty, our commute wasn't impacted by travel restrictions, and our kids never missed a day of school. With the notable exception of toilet paper, our family was minimally impacted by a world turned upside down. We even look back on those times with a certain gratitude for all that we learned and the purpose we felt during a time of relative uncertainty.

But it's not only during times of crisis that the family economy shines. The family has always been a "bulwark of liberty"—the first line of defense against hostile influences and corrupt ideologies that would undo innocence and weaken bonds. But a family can be a fortress only as long as it sustains itself and does not become overly dependent on foreign provision (this holds true for nation-states as well). Rebuilding the family economy, then, represents a critical step in wresting power away from invading institutions and restoring it to the home.

Faith of Our Fathers

Perhaps most vitally, the family economy means discipleship. Over the course of working together for several years, I noticed how the most important conversations I had with my children always came with a pitchfork in my hand (or a hammer, or a t-post). It wasn't at church or in the living room or even around the dinner table that most of these moments presented themselves. It was while we worked together.

All of the gifted teachers and Sunday school lessons cannot suffice for time together in the "little church" that is your home. Time is the critical component. There are many valuable skills to be learned in a home-based business, but none of them are eternal. It is what the family economy enables that matters most: transmitting our faith, culture, and values to the next generation.

A PROVEN PATH

These are a few of the benefits we discovered in our family as we began to work together. It didn't happen all at once, and there were certainly missteps along the way. But the course of our lives is forever changed. I can say that the family economy, though ancient, remains a proven path. It provides real solutions to the stated consequences of industrialism and opens the way to healing for fragmented families of today.

To summarize, the family economy:

1. Rebuilds Marriages, by aligning vision for husband and wife

2. Welcomes Children, by creating purpose and place for each one

3. Refunctionalizes Homes, by restoring traditional household functions back into the home

4. Creates Resilience, by fostering dependence on each other, and our local communities, rather than on external interests

5. Cultivates Faith, by enabling mentorship, apprenticeship, and discipleship at home

In the end, our efforts toward a family economy reframed our entire understanding of economy, and for that matter, family. Work was no longer just a means to a paycheck, with the mode of work prioritized according the size of that paycheck. Work was a means to relationship. Time, not money, became our primary motivation. And it is a compensation package I have never regretted.

3

Work, Worship, Wisdom

A familie is a little Church, and a little commonwealth . . .
—WILLIAM GOUGE, 1622

A FAMILY ECONOMY IS many things. It is everything a family does that makes up the life of that family. In this way, it evades common definition: each family economy may appear markedly different from another, and markedly different within the same family as the years and seasons unfold. But at its core, the family economy consists of three elements which are shared by all. They are work, worship, and wisdom.

Work provides for the body. Worship nurtures the soul. And wisdom speaks to the mind. Like legs of a stool or pillars of a foundation, all three of these stabilizing forces must be present to ensure a viable family economy. All three must be engaged to turn the tide of disunion.

The family that labors together and grows a thriving business but does not worship together will succeed only in storing up treasures that moth and rust destroy, winning perishable crowns while forsaking the eternal. The family that worships together and educates its own children but spends the rest of its time in divided labor and split vision will succeed in instilling spiritual ideals with no practical form. Their children will grow up and have no other choice but to find livelihoods in the world—livelihoods which are unlikely to conform to the spiritual ideals of their parents.

The writing is on the wall, and has been for a long time. If there is anything to be salvaged from the mounting wreckage of modernity, it will be parents who understand the times and take it upon themselves to begin preparing for the future reality now.

So let's begin.

WORK

We eat together, we rest together, we recreate together. We attend church on Sunday together. But it is work that occupies the central focus of our time. "Six days shalt thou labour," the commandment reads. So foundational was the family economy to common life in ancient Israel that embedded within the commandment on labor and rest is the expectation that sons and daughters would be found working alongside their parents: "But the seventh day is a Sabbath to the LORD your God. On it you shall not do any work, you, or your son, or your daughter . . ."[29] The Decalogue, in other words, was written to households, not individuals.

From Adam and Eve who kept a garden to Abraham, Isaac, and Jacob who herded sheep in successive generations to Joseph who tended flocks with his brothers to Elisha who plowed his family's fields to Jesus, the carpenter's son: biblical

29. Exod 20:9–10.

precedent and thousands of years of historical practice make it clear that God intended families to work together.[30] It would follow that there is a blessing inherent when families attempt to join together in this way.

"An ax head by itself is of little use to take down trees," writes Kevin Swanson. "Place an ax head on an ax handle, and the capability for useful work has increased a hundred fold. This demonstrates the basic elements of the family economy as designed by God."[31]

Start Small but Start Somewhere

I do not recommend that anyone quit their job and buy an alpaca farm. At least not right away. We didn't fall into our current predicament overnight, and we're probably not going to get out of it overnight, either. It took generations to lose our way; it might take some time to recover it. But don't let that dissuade you from starting.

Rebuilding the family economy is a gradual process; it is laying a new foundation, one brick at a time. Start by assessing the individual strengths of each member of your family. Use the Family Gifts Inventory in Part II as a guide. Then consider how all of these gifts might combine into a shared family vision. For some, that might involve starting a new home-based business. For others, it might mean moving to the country and learning to homestead. For those whose hearts have been turned to their children, it might mean walking away from a higher-paying job in order to spend more time with their families. A simple place to start

---

30. Gen 2:15–25; 12:4–5; 26:12–14; 30:43; 37:2; 1 Kgs 19:19–20; Mark 6:3.

31. Swanson, *Family Life*, 113.

is growing food: reduce your need for an income by supplying more of what you need at home (and increase your independence in the process).

The point is to start somewhere, and do it together. And see if God does not bless your efforts as you join together in "one heart and one way."[32]

When we started writing a family newsletter several years ago, we had no idea where it would lead. We just knew that it was something we could do together. We wrote mostly about farming, family, and faith, and how those topics fit together quite well. The kids contributed articles and Becca and I offered reflections on what we were learning from life in the country. We printed it and sent it out to a few dozen friends and family. From there it spread by word-of-mouth to hundreds more, and we soon started receiving letters from other families who were building their own economies (which we share about in our newsletters).

All that writing led to a book, *Durable Trades*—an inquiry into historical, family-centered professions that can still provide a living today. The book led to more writing and speaking opportunities. We hosted workshops on our farm and invited friends we had made through the book and newsletter. These events birthed a ministry geared towards helping other families to build their own economies. The ministry, Gather & Grow, focuses on gathering like-minded families, encouraging them, and equipping them with resources—such as the one you are reading.

Our family economy currently consists of farming, writing, and teaching. But I don't expect that to remain static. A family economy is never static; that's what makes it so

32. Jer 32:39.

exciting. Ask us a year from now and there'll likely be a new enterprise springing forth, likely spearheaded by one of our children—a woodworking shop, a children's book, a pop-up bakery, a flower boutique—as we grow and experiment and discern the gifts of our family.

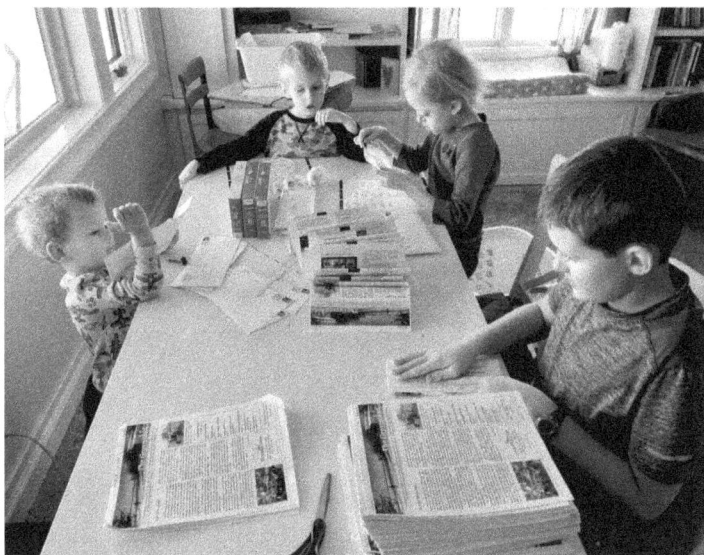

The Early Years: Folding and Stuffing. (Photo: Rory Groves)

Our newsletter, *The Grovestead*, now mails to over three thousand families, reaching all fifty states and five continents. *Durable Trades* has been read by thousands more. Our homesteading events consistently sell out—in fact, space is a pressing issue—and we are looking into ways to host gatherings in other locales.

If you were to tell me that our little family newsletter would one day lead to a new career, I would never have believed you. But that's exactly what happened. We made relationships, not income, the goal. We sought for ways to work together, ways that fit our family's gifts and honored God. And then we took the first step. The rest, as they say, is history.

But our experience is not unique. One of the most rewarding aspects of this career has been hearing the success stories of other families. In the few short years since we started, we have heard from numerous families whose part-time side-hustles turned into viable careers, who miraculously found land to begin a homestead, or whose income *increased* after switching to more family-conducive jobs. These are just a few examples of blessings inherent in family-centered work.

So discern your calling, make relationship the priority, then put your hand to the plow and don't look back.

WORSHIP

Worship represents the sacred dimension of your family economy, that which nourishes the soul. It is something that every family can do, starting today. Worship does not require any special skills or equipment. It is perhaps the simplest step you can take and by far the most important.

If I could say nothing else, it would be this: A family economy begins on your knees. You don't need land or a farm to have a family economy. What you need is vision, and conviction: Your family is not a random collection of individuals pursuing their own separate ends. You were joined together by God. And he has a unique purpose for your family that no other family on Earth can accomplish, because no other family is exactly like yours.

Worship brings your family into the center of God's will, and true life-sustaining vision can only be found there. Faith formation is not the delegated responsibility of the youth group pastor. Every father is the priest of his home and should lead his family in daily worship. Though the practice has largely been forgotten, or ignored, in modern times, reformers through the ages spoke of its import to church and family life. They warned that if family worship was ever neglected, it would necessarily lead to the crumbling of the church—and society. Says author and pastor Joel Beeke,

> As goes family worship, so goes the home. As goes the home, so goes the church. As goes the churches, so goes the nation. My leading of family worship, in my family, is the most important thing I do in this world.[33]

Sing, Study, Pray

Family worship may include many things, and each family will practice it differently depending on the age—and attention span—of its members. But it includes, at a minimum, singing, reading the Scriptures, and prayer. Find a hymn book or make your own with "psalms and hymns and spiritual songs." Our first 'family hymnal' was a collection of a dozen or so hymns that we wanted our children to know. If anyone plays an instrument, encourage them to learn the tunes and play along. Then read a chapter from the Bible and discuss it. Dads do not need to sermonize, but they should share from the heart what God is impressing upon them from *this scripture*, at *this hour*. Then call out to God together

---

33. See Beeke's excellent guide, *Family Worship*.

to refresh your family, to repent of misdeeds, and commit your work to him, that "your plans will be established."[34]

Family worship is a space for reflection and connection, a time for souls to be tended. We disciple while we work and inspire while we teach, but it is during worship that our hearts are laid bare. Worship is the heartbeat of our day, a time to take the pulse of our family, to discover what is bothering your children or your spouse: spiteful words, hidden fears, deceiving spirits, or secret sins. I can always tell when something is amiss in my family when we sit down to worship together. And I will, as the occasion warrants, correct, reprove, or encourage my flock. Sometimes, I am the one repenting, or the one in need of encouragement. And surrounded by my family, under the fervent prayers of my wife, my sons, my daughters, my armor is mended so I can face another giant.

Family worship does not need to be lengthy—twenty minutes is plenty—but it ought to be consistent and inviolable. Make it so that your children will remember one thing regardless of where they go in life: Mom and Dad prioritized the worship of God in our home.

WISDOM

Finally, wisdom represents the intellectual dimension of the family economy; that which speaks to the mind. Broadly speaking, this involves restoring the responsibility of education to the household and the role of teaching to parents. I say "restoring" because, historically, this was how all families educated their young. It wasn't until compulsory education

34. Prov 16:3.

laws began in the 1850s that teaching became a role for professionals and education the purview of the State.

The average American child today will spend sixteen thousand hours in public K-12 education.[35] It is challenging, to say the least, to construct a family-centered economy when the majority of your family is absent for the first third of their lives. More challenging still is when "substitute parents" teach doctrines contrary to ones you are instilling at home.

There are few decisions we have made as parents that have been as fruitful in our family as the decision to homeschool. The key to understanding this, I believe, is that education is inherently a moral pursuit. We as parents have the duty (I would call it privilege) of raising our children in the way they should go. Public schools, as with all factories, break apart mentor relationships in order to mass-produce. In doing so, they strip morality from education, and never the twain shall meet. One schoolteacher in front of thirty students for one hour a day cannot possibly be expected to convey the moral truths underpinning the subject she is trying to teach—nor is she legally permitted to do so. But parents cannot help but mentor as they teach. They are living textbooks, studied day and night, full of promise and short on perfection. Truth, love, failure, and forgiveness reside within every home. It's all part of an authentic education, and parents make for fine tutors.

35. State Education Practices, "Table 1.1: Minimum number of instructional days and hours."

To Train Up A Child

I concede that not every family is in a position to allow one parent to stay home. But more often than not I have observed that it doesn't come down to finances but rather fear that prevents families from taking this essential step—fear of opinions, fear of failure, fear of giving up one's own free time. Fear, even, of extended time with one's own children. But as with all things worth having, sacrifice is involved. If one cannot, like a grain of wheat, fall to the ground and die, he can never bear fruit. He remains only a single seed. "But if it dies, it bears much fruit."[36] The key to getting past initial fears, therefore, is to focus on the fruit waiting to be borne.

If you are looking for a place to start, I would suggest visiting a homeschool group in your area or connecting with local families who have been homeschooling for a while and asking questions. Another option is attending a homeschool convention. That's how we started before any of our kids were of school age. We went unsure of whether homeschooling would fit our family or if we could even make it work. We came away inspired by the teachings we heard and the families we met, many of whom we still count as dear friends.

Regardless of who is teaching your children, the primary responsibility for education rests with parents. In particular, it rests with fathers: "Fathers, do not provoke your children to anger, but bring them up in the discipline and instruction of the Lord."[37] The goal of education is not academic achievement or vocational success. It is certainly not college admission. The object of education is to preserve the

36. John 12:24.
37. Eph 6:4.

42

wisdom of past generations—the moral wealth of inherited knowledge—and in so doing, train our children in the way they should go. And this is most likely to happen at home.

SMALL BEGINNINGS

Vision comes from God and sets our hands to work. Through work we provide for our bodies and challenge our minds. By wisdom we discover the world and our place in it. And the knowledge accumulated becomes an inheritance, even, to our children's children.

Work, worship, and wisdom. Each can be practiced individually, and individual benefits will accrue. But when combined under a single household, a new family economy is born—and it is a force to be reckoned with. Households of past eras understood and practiced this. They were familiar with supply shortages, encroaching bureaucracies, and "barbarians at the gate." The productive household provided real security in times of trouble—such as those we are now entering.

As previously mentioned, the solution to these challenges can only come from families and they can only start at home. Social science has demonstrated what we all instinctively know: that parents who fail to bond with their children are more likely to raise adults who, if they have children at all, have difficulty bonding with them as well.[38] Many fractures in the modern family can be traced back to parents who, a generation ago, decided to leave the path and place ambition ahead of their family's well-being.

---

38. Komisar, *Being There*.

Conversely, research shows that parents who are present and engaged with their children, especially in the early years, are more likely to raise adults who successfully bond with their children—bonds that signal the flourishing of that family. They are more likely to raise siblings who remain loyal and lasting friends. Siblings that turn into kin networks who support each other in hard times, preserve the faith of their fathers, and withstand the centrifugal forces of a self-absorbed culture.

Rebuilding the family economy represents a "generational pivot" away from the flood of dissipation toward a unified whole: the family as it was designed to work. Regardless of the family you came from, whether broken or whole, we all have it in our power to chart a new course with our own families. If you do nothing but continue in the Way of Cain, you can be assured the rising tide will "break down all opposition"—every last relationship. But if you act, you can change the course of one family. One family who will, in time, change the course of empires.

What therefore God has joined together, let not man put asunder.

PART II

Practice

1

Family Gifts Inventory

*What Could Your Family Do Together That You
Could Never Do Apart?*

The Family Gifts Inventory is a simple exercise to help you
build your family economy by discovering the unique *gifts,
interests, education,* and *experience* of each member, and how
these traits might fit together into a shared family enterprise.

We created this exercise for our first Grovestead Gathering event to help families broaden their imaginations and
brainstorm new ideas for their own economies. We have
received more positive feedback about this activity than any
other we've done. We hope it is helpful for you as well.

The writing prompts will take about five to seven minutes per person, plus additional time to discuss ideas. Set
aside at least thirty to forty-five minutes. For larger families
it will take longer.

INSTRUCTIONS

1. Call a Family Meeting

Gather your family together for a discussion time. Begin with prayer: ask God to reveal his will for your family. Remember, you were joined together by God, and he has a unique plan for your family that no other family on Earth can accomplish, because no other family is exactly like yours.

2. Take Inventory

Next, get out a notebook and write down each family member's name on a separate sheet. Beginning with Dad, read each of the prompts below aloud and record what is shared by everyone (including Dad):

- What is Dad naturally gifted at?
- What are Dad's interests and passions?
- What is Dad's education and training? (For younger children: favorite school subjects?)
- What was Dad's favorite job or work experience? (For younger children: What would you like to do when you grow up?)

Repeat for Mom next, and then each child.

Note: Nothing shuts down a brainstorming session faster than criticism. When sharing gifts and abilities and interests, this is not a time for sarcasm or teasing. Be considerate of every idea put forth and keep an open mind to new possibilities.

3. Do the Math

Now, "do the math": What do your gifts, interests, education and experience "add up to" in a shared family enterprise?

Start with Dad and Mom, who form the foundation: What could you do together? How do your different gifts actually complement each other? Then, add your children into the equation: How might their gifts complement each idea?

Do any ideas especially stand out to you? Circle these.

Do you have resources (land, money, time, equipment) or access to resources that would make some ideas more feasible than others? Make note of this.

Don't worry about replacing your income right now. The goal of this exercise is to find modes of work that bring your family together and play to your strengths as a "work unit." Let time, and Providence, bring the increase.

> Note: If you need help coming up with practical ideas, refer to the next exercise: "Some Ideas to Get You Started."

4. Move Forward

For each idea circled, write down the first step: What would you need to do to move this idea forward?

Sometimes the way forward is stepping back. A healthy family economy is as much about what you cut out as what you add in. Do hobbies, entertainment, social commitments, or extracurricular activities need to be curtailed in order to free up more time for family endeavors? Do hours or responsibilities at work need to be renegotiated to allow more time at home?

It is important not to try to figure out how it all works out in the end. That would be walking "by sight" and not "by faith." Trust me, God has a better plan for your family than you can possibly imagine. Just focus on prayerfully taking the first step and trust God to reveal the second.

Close out your time with prayer again. Ask the Lord to "establish the work of your hands" (Ps 90:17). And then, step forward in faith.

Godspeed!

2

Ideas to Get You Started

WHEN I FINISHED WRITING *Durable Trades*, we hired a babysitter and I took my wife out for dinner at our favorite Thai restaurant. Over cream cheese wontons we thumbed through each trade in the manuscript and discussed which ones might fit our family.

Becca was my closest confidant during the research and writing stages. She and I had shared many late-night conversations about the future direction of our family. We were fully aware of the challenges ahead—the same challenges discussed here. So our discussion of career and life goals that evening took on a special significance. We were both committed to making a change, and making it urgently.

I wanted to leave you a list of possibilities that you can thumb through, after you both have had a chance to read this book and discuss it. Possibilities that have worked for other families through the ages and still work today. May this list spur some fruitful conversations and grease-stained pages for you as well.

25 MOST FAMILY-CENTERED TRADES[39]

1. *Shepherd (Animal Husbandry)* - Raising animals for food (beef/chicken/pork/lamb/dairy/honey), fiber, pets, or as breeding stock. Dog breeding is a proven business in many family economies.

2. *Farmer* - Raising vegetable crops for wholesale markets (a staple in plain communities); community-supported agriculture (CSAs), U-pick orchards and berry farms, raising specialty crops, such as microgreens or certified-organic; conventional crop-farming if you have access to land and equipment.

3. *Woodworker* - Hand-crafted furniture; custom cabinetry; finish carpentry; hand-made toys, utensils, and decor.

4. *Gardener* - Landscaping and lawn maintenance; arborist and tree care; cut flowers; plant starts; seed saving and sales; tree, shrub and nursery sales; garden consultation services.

5. *Tailor* - Weaving; dressmaking; tailoring and alterations.

6. *Silversmith* - Jeweler; jewelry-making.

7. *Author* - Professional writing; copywriting; writing fiction or non-fiction books; independent journalism.

8. *Publisher* - Traditional publishing is slowly dying but there are still opportunities for small-scale publishers on niche topics, particularly in digital formats such as e-books and podcasting.

39. This list is adapted from *Durable Trades*, which incorporates several other factors in its rankings, such as historical stability, resistance to automation, and barriers to entry. This ranking is based solely on the Family Centeredness score.

9. *Musician* - Musically inclined families may find opportunities in performing or producing albums.

10. *Winemaker* - Viticulture is a long-standing family profession that incorporates all stages of agriculture and yields a harvest that never spoils. Some family-run wineries in Europe have operated continuously since the tenth century AD.

11. *Midwife or Doula* - Though limited mostly to women, midwifery has enjoyed a significant resurgence in recent years and may provide a substantial revenue stream to those families for whom it works.

12. *Innkeeper* - The centerpiece of many successful family economies is a rental property or home-sharing property (or properties) on AirBnB or VRBO platforms.

13. *Artist* - Gifted painters and sculptors enjoy a limited but loyal clientele, and nearly all of their work is at home. A modern rendition is graphic illustration and design, which has no shortage of demand.

14. *Butcher* - It's been years since the pandemic disrupted our food supply and meat processors are still teeming with business. Though initial outlays are steep, custom processing is a highly stable trade that isn't going anywhere.

15. *Sawyer* - Custom dimensional-lumber milling; mobile milling; kiln-drying (ideally paired with logging and woodworking).

16. *Carpenter* - Construction affords nearly limitless opportunities, particularly with reputable builders, though children's involvement is more limited.

17. *Leatherworker* - Apparel and accessories; custom, hand-crafted leatherworks.

18. *Cook* - Caterer; restaurateur; specialty boutiques like cupcake shops or food trucks.

19. *Armorer (Gunsmith)* - There are over 400 million guns in America. Somebody needs to service them.

20. *Metalsmith (Machinist, Welder, Metalworker)* - Custom machining and metalworking trades enjoy heavy demand regardless of economic cycles. Often such outfits can be operated from home garages or sheds.

21. *Baker* - Cottage food laws in many states now permit the sale of uninspected, homemade pastry products to consumers—a great low-capital, work-from-home option for the confectionery-inclined.

22. *Painter* - With minimal startup costs and resistance to automation and recession, skilled interior and exterior painters enjoy a lucrative career that is always in demand.

23. *Tutor* - Private instruction enjoys a large and growing market, and there are numerous opportunities to teach what you know from home.

24. *Minister* - Plant a church, mission, or gospel-centered ministry with your family.

25. *Counselor (Consultant, Advisor, Coach)* - Share the specialized wisdom and understanding you have spent a lifetime acquiring.

3

Additional Resources

I SELECTED THE FOLLOWING resources because they have had a tremendous impact on the shaping of our family—of our understanding of historical events that led to the breakdown of the family—and how to rebuild it.

FURTHER READING

Family Economy

- *Durable Trades: Family-Centered Economies That Have Stood the Test of Time* by Rory Groves (Front Porch Republic, 2020).

- *The Grovestead Newsletter*—Our family's quarterly print newsletter on the topics of faith, family, and farming (gatherandgrow.us).

- *The Natural Family: A Manifesto* by Allan C. Carlson and Paul T. Mero (Spence, 2009)

- *The Natural Family Where It Belongs: New Agrarian Essays* by Allan C. Carlson (Routledge, 2014)

- *Family Life: A Simple Guide to the Biblical Family* by Kevin Swanson (Generations, 2016)

- *Man of the House: A Handbook for Building a Shelter That Will Last in a World That Is Falling Apart* by C. R. Wiley (Resource, 2017)

- *Family Worship* by Joel R. Beeke (Reformation Heritage, 2002)

- *Education: Does God Have an Opinion?* by Israel Wayne (Master, 2017)

Industrialism, Modernity, and Collapse

- *Rebels against the Future: The Luddites and Their War on the Industrial Revolution* by Kirkpatrick Sale (Addison-Wesley, 1995)

- *Culture, Agriculture, and the Land* by Blair Adams (Colloquium, 2008)

- *The Unsettling of America: Culture and Agriculture* by Wendell Berry (Counterpoint, 2004)

- *Haven in a Heartless World: The Family Besieged* by Christopher Lasche (Basic, 1979)

- *Uncivilisation: The Dark Mountain Manifesto* by Paul Kingsnorth and Dougald Hine (2009)

Historical Family Life

- *Family and Civilization* by Carle C. Zimmerman (Regnery, 2008)

- *The Puritan Family: Religion and Domestic Relations in Seventeenth-Century New England* by Edmund S. Morgan (Harper & Row, 1966)

- *A Little Commonwealth: Family Life in Plymouth Colony* by John Demos (Oxford, 2000)

AUDIO RECORDINGS

We have numerous audio recordings on the topics presented in this book—family economy, discipleship, homesteading, and community preparedness—recorded at conferences we have hosted with various speakers. Please visit our website to learn more: gatherandgrow.us/resources

BULK PURCHASES

Discounted copies of this book for church or group studies are available on our website: gatherandgrow.us.

CONNECT WITH US

If you are building a new family economy, or looking to connect with others who are doing so, we'd like to hear from you. Gather & Grow is a Christian ministry dedicated to rebuilding the family economy—we exist to help families like yours. We publish resources and host events with the goal of encouraging Christian families in the Lord. Contact us at gatherandgrow.us, or write to: Gather & Grow Ministries, PO Box 326, Northfield, MN 55057.

Afterword
Homecoming

You have seen the darkness. The light now summons you. . . .
You have the ability to craft a true homecoming. Your genera-
tion holds the destiny of humankind in its hands. The hopes of
all good and decent people lie with you.
— THE NATURAL FAMILY

FOR NEARLY FIFTY YEARS, I have attempted to describe, understand, and respond to the family crisis afflicting the nations we once, almost quaintly, saw as forming "Christian Civilization." The symptoms of disorder have been clear: falling fertility rates, reflecting a retreat from childbearing, linked in turn to aggressive contraception and widespread abortion; a rejection of marriage by ever growing numbers of young adults; ever later "age of first marriage" and a high divorce rate among those who do marry; the remarkable surrender of parental rights to public schools and other state entities; and the cultural normalization and legal embrace of the sterile lifestyles.

Many attempts have been made to ascribe the cause, or causes, of this social and moral revolution. Explanations that have been offered include secularization, or a broad retreat from Christian faith; equity feminism, or the deliberate negation of all biological, cultural, and economic differences between men and women; sexual revolution, which has sought to obliterate any meaningful connection between the sexual act and procreation; and openly hostile political ideologies such as socialism or communism.

Near the end of this personal effort (I say "near the end" for I am of relatively advanced age), I can now report that none of these arguments really works. In every case, the purported "cause" of the family crisis actually is but a symptom of the problem under review.

The true cause is to be found elsewhere: in the deliberate destruction of the home economy by the industrial principle! Prior to the industrial revolution launched a little over two hundred years ago, the family household was the center of most productive activities. Each family raised most of its own food, made most of its own clothing, provided most of its own fuel, crafted most of its own furniture, built its own shelter, and so on. Even children found productive places in the barnyard and fields. As anthropologist Hugh Brody has summarized, "Everyday is long and filled with the activities of the family . . . . There is a loyalty . . . to the tasks and expertise and duties that each member of the family undertakes . . . . The family in the farm is the family where it belongs."[1]

The industrial principle focused on centralization and the quest for efficiency tore through this settled and humane way of life. The family household ceased to be the center of

1. Brody, "Nomads and Settlers," 3.

productive labor and loyalty. Centralized factories, warehouses, and offices displaced home workshops, gardens, and storehouses. Cash exchanges pushed aside the altruistic bonds of the family. Industrialization destroyed the ancient unity of home and work, the natural ecology of the family, which had prevailed for thousands of years. Mothers, fathers, and children alike were pulled into, and separated by, the wage-labor market. Family bonds, once the source of economic strength, now stood as obstructions to the efficient allocation of labor, The individual, unencumbered and alone, was the new ideal worker. In this regime, secularism, feminism, sexual disorder, and the various forms of socialism all served the industrial principle.

So, what should be done? Sixteen years ago, my colleague Paul Mero and I sought to give answers in our book, *The Natural Family: A Manifesto.* Why use the adjective "natural" here? At a simple and direct level, it refers back to the Universal Declaration of Human Rights, adopted by the United Nations in 1948, in response to the moral disorders that had led to World War II. In its Article 16(c), this document declares that "the family is the natural and fundamental group unit of society, entitled to protection by society and the state."[2] Other provisions of this powerful declaration affirm that the family builds on heterosexual marriage and a commitment to the bearing and rearing of children. At a more philosophical—even theological—level, the adjective "natural" affirms that true marriage and family is grounded in human nature, the created order, and cannot be altered by human whim.

---

2. United Nations, "Universal Declaration of Human Rights." https://www.un.org/en/about-us/universal-declaration-of-human-rights.

Facing our age of moral disorder and mounting human casualties, this Manifesto offered a fairly simple and clear program of action:

- We will build a new culture of marriage;
- We will welcome and celebrate more babies and larger families;
- We will find ways to bring mothers, fathers, and children back home; and
- We will create true home economies!

As Groves explains in this study, the fourth principle ably engages and gives substance to the first three. The marriage of a man and a woman is the foundation of every true home. The appearance of children brings fulfillment to the promise of marriage and the Divine command that the married couple be "fruitful and multiply." And the operation of household-centered enterprises repairs the vast damages of the industrial revolution.

Those who seek a way forward in the cultural anarchy of the contemporary age should focus on this clear imperative: build a viable home economy!

In the end, it is that simple.

Allan C. Carlson
October 2023

Acknowledgments

WOODROW WILSON WAS ONCE asked how long it took him to prepare his speeches. "It depends," he said. "If I am to speak for ten minutes, I will need a week to prepare. If I am to speak for thirty minutes, I'll need two days. If I am to speak for an hour, I am ready now." So it is with writing a short book. Condensing this important topic into the fewest possible pages proved to be a gargantuan task—one that I did not expect—and one that I could not have finished without critical support along the way.

My deepest gratitude goes to Allan Carlson and Jared Dodd: partners in rebuilding the family economy. To James Stock and the team at Wipf & Stock, thank you for taking another chance. To Evan Birdsong for editorial support, book recommendations, and many-hatted conversations. To our readers, guests, and supporters of Gather & Grow: you inspire us to keep going—this book would not exist without you!

To Ivar, Elsie, Hattie, Alden, Elias, and Abel: you are the reason I write.

And to Becca, for your extraordinary patience and faith. You are my whole world.

Bibliography

Allen, Frederick. *The Shoe Industry*. New York: Henry Holt, 1922.

American Antiquarian Society. "Situation of the Lowell Girls." *Dwight's American Magazine and Family Newspaper*, April 11, 1846. https://americanantiquarian.org/millgirls/items/show/60.

———. "Who Were the Mill Girls?" *Mill Girls in Nineteenth-Century Print*. Fall 2015. https://americanantiquarian.org/millgirls/exhibits/show/culture/culture/who.

Beeke, Joel R. *Family Worship*. Grand Rapids: Reformation Heritage, 2002.

Berry, Wendell. *The World-Ending Fire: The Essential Wendell Berry*. Berkley: Counterpoint, 2017.

Bly, Robert. *Iron John: A Book about Men*. New York: Vintage, 1990.

Brody, Hugh. "Nomads and Settlers." In *Town and Country*, edited by Anthony Barnett and Roger Scruton. London: Jonathan Cape, 1998.

Bureau of Labor Statistics. *History of Wages in the United States from Colonial Times to 1928*. October 1929. https://fraser.stlouisfed.org/title/4126.

Carlson, Allan C. *Family Cycles: Strength, Decline, and Renewal in American Domestic Life*. New York: Routledge, 2017.

Carlson, Allan C., and Paul T. Mero. "The Natural Family: A Manifesto." *Family in America* 19.3, Special Edition (2005).

CDC. "Facts about Suicide." National Vital Statistics System, Mortality 2018–2021, 2023. https://www.cdc.gov/suicide/facts/index.html.

Demos, John. *A Little Commonwealth: Family Life in Plymouth Colony*. Oxford: Oxford University Press, 2000.

Engels, Frederick. *The Principles of Communism*. In *Selected Works*, translated by Paul Sweezy, 1:81–97. Moscow: Progress, 1969 https://www.marxists.org/archive/marx/works/1847/11/prin-com.htm.

Hauerwas, Stanley, and William H. Willimon. *Resident Aliens: Life in the Christian Colony*. Nashville: Abingdon, 1989.

Institute for Health Metrics and Evaluation. "Global Burden of Disease." 2023. https://www.healthdata.org/research-analysis/gbd.

Jefferson, Thomas. *Notes on the State of Virginia*, Query XIX. 1782. https://en.wikisource.org/wiki/Notes_on_the_State_of_Virginia_(1853)/Query_19.

Komisar, Erica. *Being There: Why Prioritizing Motherhood in the First Three Years Matters.* New York: TarcherPerigee, 2017.

McCloskey, Deirdre. Review of *The Cambridge Economic History of Modern Britain,* edited by Roderick Floud and Paul Johnson. *Times Higher Education Supplement,* Jan 15, 2004. http://deirdremccloskey.org/articles/floud.php.

McKenzie, Robert Tracy. "How the Pilgrims' Story Might Challenge and Convict Us." *Faith and American History,* Nov 22, 2017. https://faithandamericanhistory.wordpress.com/2017/11/22/how-the-pilgrims-story-might-challenge-and-convict-us-2/.

Mumford, Lewis. *The Myth of the Machine.* Vol. 2, *The Pentagon of Power.* New York: Harcourt, 1967.

National Bureau of Economic Research. "Total Cotton Production by Mills in New England." *St. Louis Fed,* last updated Nov 1, 2019. https://alfred.stlouisfed.org/series?seid=CPNETOTAL#0.

Petrusich, Amanda. "Going Home with Wendell Berry." *New Yorker,* Jul 14, 2019. https://www.newyorker.com/culture/the-new-yorker-interview/going-home-with-wendell-berry.

Rice-Oxley, Mark. "Mental Illness: Is There Really a Global Epidemic?" *The Guardian,* Jun 3, 2019. https://www.theguardian.com/society/2019/jun/03/mental-illness-is-there-really-a-global-epidemic.

Robinson, Harriet. *Loom and Spindle.* New York: Thomas Y. Cromwell, 1898.

Schaeffer, Francis. *True Spirituality.* Wheaton: Tyndale House, 2001.

Shammas, Carole. "The Decline of Textile Prices in England and British America Prior to Industrialization." *The Economic History Review* 47.3 (1994): 483–507. https://doi.org/10.2307/2597590.

State Education Practices. "Table 1.1: Minimum number of instructional days and hours in the school year, minimum number of hours per school day, and school start/finish dates, by state: 2020." National Center for Education Statistics, 2020. https://nces.ed.gov/programs/statereform/tab1_1-2020.asp.

Swanson, Kevin. *Family Life: A Simple Guide to the Biblical Family.* Colorado: Generations, 2016.

Thoreau, Henry David. "Inspiration." Poets.org. Academy of American Poets. https://poets.org/poem/inspiration.

———. *Walden, or, Life in the Woods.* Boston: Ticknor and Fields, 1854.

Wiley, C. R. "Against the Recreational Household." Speech, August 27, 2021, recorded at The Grovestead Farm, Minnesota.

Zimmerman, Carle C. *Family and Civilization.* Washington: Regnery, 2008.

www.ingramcontent.com/pod-product-compliance
Lightning Source LLC
LaVergne TN
LVHW041203080426
835511LV00006B/720